AF545056

The Right Amount of Sunshine:

Cultivating Little Girls into Young Ladies

The Right Amount of Sunshine

Brenda's Child for Two-Two INK

ISBN 978-0-557-52514-0

Rosebuds

Little girls are like roses,
Beautiful, but delicate,
In unfavorable conditions,
Even through weeds and cement
Their growth is imminent

But our roses can thrive and fully bloom
If they are properly nourished.
Plant them with values,
Water them with self-esteem,
Shine the right amount of light,
And watch them flourish!

Introduction

I know what you're thinking, I am barely in my thirties, what am I doing writing a memoir? I haven't lived; I still have so much life left, right? Well, that's not necessarily true; we never know when our time is up. My mother died when she was just twenty-three years old. She never had a chance to raise her two daughters, or discover her true calling.

As a result, when I turned eighteen, an intense fear crept into my heart. Would I be doomed to leave this earth before I had a chance to live out my purpose? Her situation was rare; she developed a malignant form of breast cancer. I had always heard that cancer was hereditary, what if I got it? This thought plagued me until my twenty-fourth birthday. I had outlived my mother, and when I looked at where I was in life it saddened me. I had just recently come to the realization that my purpose was to work with young people and began my first salaried position in the field of human services. What if I died the year before? I felt like she was cheated.

It took me a long time to realize that only God knows what's supposed to happen, when and why. Once I accepted this, I made up my mind that I would live for both of us, which meant I had to really live life to its fullest. Although Brenda Kay Swinton's journey ended prematurely, in the four short years she nurtured me, she was able to leave an indelible impression on my spirit. This mark has been a driving force for what has become my mission. So this memoir is more of a reflection of my trials and tribulations, and what I have learned from them as a woman.

Each chapter begins with an actual diary entry written when I was between the ages of fourteen and seventeen, and it is completely unedited and totally dated. The names of course, have been changed to protect the innocent (and the guilty). This was a difficult period for me because not only was I undergoing puberty, but I was still struggling with the death of my maternal grandmother, Ga-Ga, who had been raising me since my mother's passing. It took a great deal of courage for me to share my private thoughts with the world because even as I typed them over from my loose leaf notebooks onto my laptop, I could remember every emotion vividly. In an instant, I was taken back to a time when filled with doubt, fear, insecurity, excitement, and chance, and I got mixed feelings. On one hand, I thought, "Wow, I had some issues!" Then I looked at the self-aware, resilient, and ambitious woman I have become, and realized that I had to experience life, in order to *impact* lives.

Some of my entries will alarm you, and I know because reading them as an adult bothered me. Some you will connect with immediately and you might even feel nostalgia (or shame). Whatever the case, I shed my layers and tell my story because I strongly believe that someone out there needs to read it.

I end each chapter with advice for parents, caregivers, teachers, and anyone who encounters our delicate little flowers. I am not a psychologist, and my name doesn't have suffix of PhD (as of yet), but I have more than a decade underneath my (studded) belt of working with youth as a mentor, service provider, and teacher. Just as important as my professional knowledge is my personal experience with the some of the same situations in which many of our young girls are struggling to thrive in.

It is my hope that after reading this book, that we begin to examine the way we speak and behave towards our young girls as they awkwardly, but amazingly grow into young ladies. I encourage anyone who isn't blessed enough to have girls around them, to find one to mentor and support. I am a living example of the power that a little positive interaction can go a long way.

Eternally,

Brenda's Child

To all my little Rosebuds

And

For my Ga-Ga,

Thanks for being
My roots, water & sunshine

Table of Contents

Time to Shine

July 24, 1994 11:55 pm
Dear Diary,

Tomboy made their official debut as a dance group tonight at the Marriot. We did Mc Hammer, "Pumps in a Bump." And it was hot. We had on our alternate black and white. Some black t-shirts with white shorts, and some had on black shorts with white shirts. I thought they were gonna think the part where we did the splitz was nasty, but they loved it! We are gonna start performing everywhere now, talent shows, everything. But anyway......

11:15 pm July 13, 1995
Dear Di,

We did great in the show! Excellent! All of the hard work was worth it. Everybody was yelling and screaming "Go Tomboy, Go Tomboy!" We didn't miss a beat. We finally pulled it together after all of the practice. I can't wait 'til tomorrow, because if they thought tonight was hot, wait 'til they see us do reggae and the tootsie roll. I thought the other group was gonna do better, but they didn't. I can't wait to rock it on Saturday...

Sept. 7, 1995 7:44 pm

Dear Diary,

I am the happiest I've been in a long time. Life is great. For starters, I am the captain of the drill team. We are about to turn it out. Coach said I can incorporate dance moves and we are looking at catalogs for uniforms. We are gonna perform at football and basketball games. We are gonna put the drill team on the map with our steppin'. I finally get to do things how I want to...creative control, they call it......

March 9, 1996

Yo, we did it! We won the all high schools dance competition. We got a huge trophy and they are gonna give us $500 to split. I was happy even though I was sick with a cold. I thought the competition was gonna be tough. Gina was in it with these girls that had on tennis skirts and they looked like they were straight out of a Mary J. Blige video, and they danced off of "Real Love." They looked good, but they messed up, and they sucked. The only competition we had was a salsa couple. But my sister was shoutin' "We won, we won!" before they even announced us as the winners. It was great! Tomboy now has proof we are the best dancers.

During the summer of 1990 and 1991, I orchestrated *Jam,* a concert held right in my backyard. I was like a miniature Debbie Allen at the introduction of *Fame*... "You want fame? Well, fame costs..." I would gather my little sister, my cousins, and my friends and at twelve, I'd put them through brutal rehearsals and choreography. We'd print and sell tickets to neighbors on surrounding streets for fifty cents. We set up rows of picnic benches, and sold ice cream cones for refreshments. One by one we'd lip sing and dance to everything from Bette Midler, to Lisa Lisa and Cult Jam. There was something about the rush of being on stage, even if it was just drive way pavement that absolutely excited me. Even today, I still love the thrill of performance: the throbbing of my heart beat before I step out, the bright lights, the roar of a satisfied audience.

I have my family to thank for always supporting me when I performed with the step squad, at dance recitals, and poetry spots. Knowing someone I loved was always watching proudly is why I never had any apprehension about being in the spotlight. I am just comfortable when all eyes are on me, which I guess is probably why I love teaching, facilitating, and reciting poetry.

I'm sure my personality type sounds familiar; every family has one, the girl who craves attention and talks incessantly.

She always has a story to tell, something to show you, or even a performance. As annoying as she may be sometimes, keep this in mind... she is speaking because she wants to be heard. If you don't listen, then she could fall victim to the first manipulative, potentially dangerous person that does pretend to listen. Even worse, she could begin the detrimental cycle of doing negative things to get that attention.

As a teacher in alternative programs, I have seen young ladies attach themselves to the first guy who shows them attention. We all know what happens after that. Unfortunately, she becomes trapped, because she was just prey to begin with. No male, young or old desires someone who is desperately in need of attention, unless he intends to use it to his advantage. On a personal level, I watched a young man seek out these types of women with the purpose of making them feel valued. His ultimate objective was for her to look to him only for validation. Once this was accomplished, he could then control her; after all, she was nothing without him. Sounds sick, huh? But this is reality.

We all lead busy lives. In today's world, many of us juggle two jobs, parenting, and extracurricular activities, and the truth is that sometimes we get stressed, become short tempered, or just plain tired. That's perfectly human. Therefore, there's nothing wrong with telling your child that you need to concentrate on the road so she can tell you about "show and tell" as soon as you get home. You could even tell her to write it down so she doesn't forget it, and then read it to you later. The key thing is that you really set aside time to actively listen to your child. By doing so, you are forging an open relationship that will hopefully continue throughout those crucial adolescent years.

She will get attention one way or another, and it all begins at home. Praise can fuel pride and drive. When I was a young girl, I showed my grandmother everything. She always told me how smart I was, how talented I was. Even though my mother wasn't around, I never felt that loss as a child, thanks to my grandmother's love. Every time I received a good grade and she told me how proud she was, it made me want to work harder to please her. This goal eventually changed; I was so used to excelling that I begin to do for myself. Now of course, every situation is different, so nothing is guaranteed, but my experience has shown me some dire effects of girls not getting sufficient positive attention at home. I have seen girls who talk loudly, dress scarcely, or even play dumb just to get noticed.

I had this one young lady in my class whose father was dead and whose mother abandoned her frequently. We'll call her Violet. I could see that she liked and admired me by the way she came in the mornings even before class started, or poked her head in between classes. She had even written her phone number down and slipped it in my desk "in case" I wanted to invite her to one of my outside youth activities. She was a beautiful, bright girl, but if ever she felt I wasn't giving her enough of my time, or I was too focused on another student, she would begin to act out.

Now in some situations, ignoring negative behavior would put an end to it. With Violet, the behavior would escalate. She would flip through a magazine loudly, whisper a joke to another student about how I thought I was "all that." She would even sit inappropriately with her legs on the desk. The strangest thing was that Violet was extremely self-aware. She had once told me that she knows she has strong leadership skills but that when she gets bored, she uses those skills to instigate "drama" for her own personal excitement.

Previously, I had used plenty of strategies to deter Violet's distracting behavior. One day, I announced to the class that for the first minute of each period would be dedicated to Violet, and that everyone had to give her their full attention. Now this was highly unconventional and even risky, and I wouldn't recommend it to anyone but as I said before, I knew Violet very well. Under the extreme circumstances, and with the cooperation of my other students, I took a chance. At first, Violet pretended to be embarrassed, she smiled and laughed, "Stop looking at me." Then, the world's most beautiful smile would appear across her face, and she would behave for the reminder of the class period.

The usual consequences I had of keeping students

after school didn't work for Violet, she gladly accepted any writing assignment, and loved to stay after school with me. I cared deeply for Violet, but our relationship was truly draining, and some days, I couldn't give her what she needed, so I had ask her to leave out of my class.

One afternoon, I told her to step out into the hallway, and she refused. I really just didn't have it in me that day, so I stood in front of her desk and said, "Violet, you have until the count of three to get out of this seat, and out of my class, or there is going to be a problem." (Let me just say, I don't know what I would do, but something in me knew that Violet would move.) She got out of her seat and spewed a bunch of swears about how if I didn't want to (insert "f" word here) teach her, then fine.

I waited until the class was on break and approached her. Of course she was still upset and using the "n" word to address me. I redirected her immediately, explaining to her that she was not talking to someone off of the streets, that she was a lady, and needed to address me like it. Once she quickly changed her tone, I chastised her much like a mother would, and Violet sat silently without talking back. I informed her of her consequence then walked away.

As I sat back at my desk, completely frustrated, I thought about a dream I had about Violet two nights before. In the dream I gave her a hug and told her I understood that it had probably been a long time since she'd been hugged by an adult, and she needed that. A couple of minutes later, I saw Violet passing back and forth outside of my classroom door. I met her in the hallway and I did and said exactly what happened in my dream. Violet let me hug her and she hugged me back. Here was this seventeen year old still yearning for love, affection, and attention because she lacked it at home.

So what do we do to give our daughters the acknowledgement so many of them crave? I don't have all the answers, but I do have some common sense suggestions. For starters, support her in everything she does. If you can't be at her soccer game, send another family member or close friend; they need to see someone cheering them on. Secondly, expose your child to as many activities as possible. You see the PSA's on television all of the time about the impact sports have on a girl's self-esteem. Don't stop there, introduce them to the arts, and nature. If she doesn't like it, fine, but broaden her experience and skills set.

For us single parents, or fulltime workers and nighttime students, it's tough, but at least once a month spend one on one time with your daughter. Even if you have three, each of them should get their own time. If you don't have a daughter, spend one on one time with a child whom you know needs it. You'd be amazed at how much you find out, how much a child divulges over lunch or arts and crafts. Lastly, tell her you love her as much as possible. If she knows she's loved by you, she won't need that validation from so many others.

Save the Drama

March 25, 1994 9:27 pm

My "so-called" birthday slumber party. Yo, I'm saying, Melanie is f**ked up, and I'm gonna tell her when everybody leaves and I'm gonna let her know that it's not that me and David were messin', but she knew I liked him. What a B**ch!

F**k her! She ain't no kinda friend. I don't care if he did like her, still she didn't have to go there. I know they are in the kitchen right now. F**k them both. I am kinda hurt 'cause both of them played me. That B**ch and that Bastard. I should tell them both to get out. But then everybody will know. I am PISSED!

Toyab

Friday Night April 22, 1994 11:36 pm

Dear Di,

Me and Randy are friends. We made up that Wednesday. You know that fool can't stay mad at me for long.

As for Lisa, our friendship is over at the moment. I wrote her a fat letter telling her how stupid she was acting. I was heated because she was acting immature and ignorant. Then I didn't speak to her. This has been going on since Tuesday.

Melanie, that b**ch! I'm still mad at her . But I paid her back, I broke her and David up. They didn't even last a month. I told him how Melanie still be calling Lance, and how she told him she was pregnant just to keep him. Go Toya! Now she feels worse.

Everybody thinks I like Lance. Shena does, Shay and her sister. But I don't, we're just mad cool, like me and Randy.

Speaking of Shay, me and her got into a crazy argument at her house. See, we went to my aunt's house. She liked Pierce (from the boys and girls club.) But he likes me. He know I don't like him, so he tried to make me jealous by talking to her. Bad move because I didn't care. When my cousin told me this, I was figuring out a way to break it to Shay. So on the way home, while Shena was giving some guy the wrong number, I was about to tell her, but she started talking about how happy she was, so I lost the nerve. So after we were at her house for a while, I told her. She gonna get mad and get loud, so I did, too. She talking about I played myself and I ain't no kinda friend. You know I was like...SAVE THE DRAMA FOR YA MAMA! It ain't my fault he didn't want her, right? She shouldn't be mad 'cause I was looking out for her feelings. So when I got home, I cut her out all of my pictures and shredded all of the letters she wrote me. It ain't no thang if another friendship is down the drain, 'cause some girls are so shifty. So I got a picture for you, as you can see Shay is cut out, just like she's cut off! I'm sticking with you, Shena, and boys for friends, 'cause some girls, got to go! Just like I gotta go!

Love ToyaB

Monday, April 25

Yo,

why did me and Shay almost fight in school today about that bullsh*t that happened last week? She gonna come to school and talk about me like I wasn't there, right in front of my face. So I told her that if she had something to say, she could say it to me. She called me shady, and it was on. She made a big scene and people was trying to break us up. I wished they woulda let her go, so I coulda got in that a** real quick. But instead we had to go to mediation and talk it out. I'm so sick of chicks, I swear. This is the second friend I almost fought. Remember when I was just gonna fight Melanie? My Goodness, I'm sick of this! Anyway...

1/31/95

I Hate Beatrice! Actually it's more like envy her. Every time I like a guy, she gets him. Willie. Helena told me told that Willie slapped Beatrice, and she slapped him back. Sure I'd try to kill Willie if he ever hit me, but still I wish he cared enough to even try. He had his coat in her locker, I remember last year at the Valentine's dance he danced with her!

Then when I liked Alex for a split second, so did she. And she ended up going out with him.!

Right before I came out of class, she and Marvin were talking in the hallway. What is it she has? Some kinda magnetism that draws men to her? Why can't I ever get who I want? I like Marvin a lot. I found out he likes root beer like me. And he hates Valentine' s Day. I do, too, but only 'cause I never get anything. I want Marvin so bad but I'll never make the mistake of letting him know. Why does she always get them!?

Girls = Drama. Period. It doesn't matter what we do, at one point in time (but probably more) there will be a fight either verbally, or physically between a girl and her arch enemy, or a girl and her best friend. In some cases that may be the same person. In my experience these fights seem to almost stem from two things…jealously or boys.

When I was in early elementary school I was quiet and reserved. It wasn't until I entered a new school in 5th grade that I had my first fight. All year long I took the 6th grade girls pulling my hair on the bus because it was long and apparently it "shouldn't have been hangin' over the seat." I looked different and I was in higher level classes, so I *had* to think I was better than them. This meant that every bus ride home after school I was forced to endure relentless bullying. My strategy of course was to ignore them. For most of the year it worked. I knew it was only a twenty-minute ride, and once I got off, I'd be free from the idiots for twenty-four hours.

One day in spring I guess these girls had enough of me ignoring them. I heard them talking about me as normal, but this time they decided to pull someone else into the drama. They told another fifth grader I was talking about her. That day when I stepped off the bus, Whitney, descended and approached me. I remember the conversation like it was yesterday:

Whitney: I heard you called me a b**ch?
Me: I didn't call you a b**ch, but I did say your sneakers were ugly.
(They really were. They were denim, fake Chuck Taylor Converse with these patches all over.)
Whitney: Well, say it in my face!
Me: (stepping closer to her) I SAID…YOUR SNEAKERS…ARE UGLY!

Whitney pushed me, and our fight began at the intersection of our streets. A man walking down the street split us apart and lectured us on the importance of sisterhood. He directed us to take our behinds home. (I wish we still had that kind of adult care and intervention with our young folks today.) Just like that, it was over.

There were several effects of my first brawl. First of all, the big bad 6th grade girls caught a glimpse of the fight, so for the rest of the year, neither of them teased me again. Secondly, Whitney and I became friends the following year after we both won scholarships. She even became a part of my backyard *Jam* concerts. More than twenty years later Whitney is still an honorary family member.

The third effect was not so positive… I became a fighter. By no means was I a trouble maker, instigator, or trash talker, but once I was approached or felt threatened, I became a pit bull. I went from reserved to untamed in a matter of seconds. It didn't matter if it was a stranger or a friend, if I was backed into a corner, I would attack.

When I was twelve years old, I beat up the fifteen year old boy who lived down the street. I can't remember the circumstances, but I remember the aftermath, when his father had to pull me off of him. It then turned into one of those family affair fights because he threatened to beat my butt, and my daddy wasn't having that. (I'll discuss this later in the chapter.)

When kids are young, they seem to fight one another one moment, and go back to sharing toys the next. One of my closest and most adversarial relationships was with my best friend who lived across the street. We fought incessantly. Once it was over the cute boy who lived down the street. Another time it was because she rode my new 10-speed bike without my permission. Whether we fought indoors or my front porch, we'd be back to playing *Barbie's* or kickball the next day.

As an adult I questioned why I remained her friend

because it seemed that every chance she had to make me feel inadequate, she did. She would point out everything I lacked, from her mom's sports car that would one day be hers, to her private school, to her boobs. She would constantly remind me how her school was so much better because they had athletics and the team traveled. We often crushed on the same boys, so she had no problem letting me know I wasn't developed enough, or tall enough, or thin enough.

What I did have was the big loving family that accepted me no matter what. Had I not, I believe that toxic friendship would have broken me eventually. I guess that's why they say that if it doesn't break you, it really does make you stronger.

Today, I know that when we attack other people with comments either viciously or subtly, it is a reflection of our own insecurities. We want something they have. It's funny how we are so focused on our own perceived shortcomings, we don't realize that other people envy what we have. Even when we become adults we are still guilty of not being able to recognize our own shine because we continue to live in someone else's shadow.

This concept can seem almost impossible to drill into the head of a sprouting female who is bombarded with images, actions, and remarks that fuel her self-doubt. What happens when this goes unresolved is that these girls become *haters*. They bad mouth the ones they envy and try to block their success. Or worse, they become victims of compensation, wanting to "Keep up with the Jones's." They fill themselves up with material things to show everyone else what they have.

I've been at both ends of the spectrum, even as an adult. I've been hated on by people whom I thought were friends and it's a hurtful feeling. I couldn't understand why, but then I had to step back, and recognize that the people who truly love me will relish in my success. They won't bad mouth behind my back, sabotage me, or secretly compete against me.

On the flip side, I've had to coach myself out of wishing I had the boyfriend, the body, the car, of my friends and enemies. My life is my life, and my path is my path. Today I still have to remind myself that as long as I'm taking action towards all I want out of life, it will come to right when it is supposed to.

What's important for us to teach our girls is that jealously is not okay, but a little envy is healthy. There is a difference; jealously is called the green monster for a reason. It can manifest quickly and take over. Jealously results in unhappiness because it can lead to self-pity. Envy on the other hand, like sugar, is okay in small doses. It can fuel our motivation and light our fire for more.

Envy can breed positive results so long as the sole purpose for accomplishment is not derived from competition.

Now boys, boys are an entirely different story. Grown women today still fight over men. I think the difference between women and young teens is that girls change boyfriends like they change clothes. When I look back at my diary, I liked a new boy almost every week; so did my friends. We went from crush to crush, from loving him, to hating him. We "went out" with boys for a week to months, and we often became territorial.

Girls quickly learn unspoken social rules about dating, and are ready to spread rumors, argue, and fight if they feel someone has violated. It was my sophomore year in particular that I got into arguments over boys with friends on different occasions. All of my relationships with whom I would call my "true friends" withstood the blow outs.

Friendship is another category in which we as adults have to set the standard. Our kids will observe the type of people with whom we surround ourselves, and what they see, determines their understanding of what is acceptable. What do they need to see? They need to see that the people we classify as friends are supportive, encouraging and loving.

What is most important is that our children grow up to see positive relationships as a normalcy, not as a rarity. They are then able to make wise decisions about who to keep in their circle, and whom they should remove.

If you set the tone, and teach the values, then you won't wind up become involved in your daughter's arguments, or trying to fight her battles. Now there are some extreme circumstances, like when you're daughter is being jumped by four girls, you have to stop it. In the incident where I fought the older boy, his father told me he would whip my "ass." So, my daddy, being the protector he was, felt like he needed to address him. Well, the man got loud with my father, and it turned into to one of those big blow outs, where all of the neighbors on the street came outside. It was ugly; his wife came outside, so my aunt came outside, and it looked like a stereotypical scene from a movie. I don't fault my father for a moment, this man wasn't threatening to punish me not out of love, but out of anger and spite. Regardless, these are the situations, we want to try to avoid.

Generally, it is best to just stay out of disputes between your children and their friends. It's perfectly fine to be a listening ear, or to give honest feedback when you feel your child is in the wrong. However, it's completely inappropriate to feel like you need to defend your thirteen year old against another thirteen year old. Whether it's because of boys or jealously, in the end, some friendships will work themselves out, and others will dissolve. So do yourself a favor and step back.

Girl Power

June 3, 1994

Dear Diary,

I'm slacking off in Spanish, Biology, and Math (as usual). I'm about to change that though. First I'm getting mad extra help in Math and making up all of my assignments. I can't believe I got a 61% on my Biology quiz. I'm doing good on the next chapter, watch. In Spanish, I usually get 90's, but I've been getting low 80's. I'm getting on top of things.

I'm feeling good 'cause I won in 21 in gym class, and I beat Jerel. But he still gave me a hug afterwards. I like being close to some of the guys, like family. It makes me feel good.

Peace,

ToyaB

2:10pm 9/12/94 Study Hall

Me, Shay, Shena, Rachel, Tracy, Kiki, and Patrice got kicked out of the hotel at 2:00 in the morning. They said we were too loud, and we had to go. So we destroyed the room like rock stars, took the batteries out of the remote, spilled ranch dip all over the place, pulled the sheets off the bed. We were there for Rachel's slumber party, but we still had a blast. We ended up piling in one of Rachel's friend's car and going to her grandmothers, where we stayed up all night talking.

Today in History we were listening to interviews of ex-slaves. It was deep, I love History, and it intrigues me. That and English are my favorite subjects.

Latoya 12.27 pm

16-Sept-1994 Fri. 11:14 am

Oh yeah, what was I saying about Mike? He's all that and a bag of cheese doodles. Let me tell you about what Shay did. She told her cousin to bring Mike to the party tonight because I like him. Shay said that he didn't come to school today because his parents are out of town and he has the house to himself. Tidow, Big Baby! I wish I was there with him!!!! I hope they do go tonight. I'll be all shy and quiet. Sometimes I don't know how to act 'because if you're quiet sometimes a guy doesn't like it. And sometimes if you're loud, and you be buggin' they find that a turn off. So how about just being yourself, you ask? Well, I'm both of them, it depends on my mood. Oh well, he probably won't go to the party anyway.

12:20 am
Friday/Saturday May 19/20 1995
Dear Diary,

Even though the Pacers lost, tonight was fun. Rachel, Shay, Lisa, Shena, and Le-anne were over. And we were all trying to do Lisa and Le-anne's weaves. Rachel burned her weave ponytail in the microwave...hilarious. It was fun, we were bonding. I'm going to miss precious moments like that. I really had a blast buggin' out with them in my kitchen, and I know they all felt the same, too.

Today me and my boy Luis made bet. I have to be his slave for a day because the Pacers lost last night. I just knew Reggie was gonna win it for me, but there's always next year.

Tomorrow is the Great Adventures trip. Me and Lisa got airbrushed shirts, they say our name on the front. We gonna wear then with our white squishy pants. I hope it's fun. I think it will be.

Latoya B.

Growing up, there were some things I absolutely loved about being a girl, mainly *Barbie's*, and baby dolls. I slept with about thirteen different dolls on the end of my bed, well-dressed and groomed. Each of them had names, and feelings as far as I was concerned. If one fell off of the bed, it needed to be consoled. I could play with my black Barbie's for hours; turning bookshelves into sky rise apartments and wash cloths into canopy beds.

Then there was dance. From the first time I put on a pair of tap shoes at three, I loved to dance. I was fascinated by the glamour of sequins, tutu's, tights, and of course, stage lights. My aunts would liven up my outfits by putting bright colored ribbons in my all black shoes, just so I could stand out. For every recital I got to have my hair pressed and curled in my grandmother's kitchen, with the hot comb fresh off the stove. The final touch was shiny lip gloss, and a bit of glitter.

Dressing up was a regular for me when I was a very young child, but I always had a little tomboy in me. This meant that at the end of the day, my tights had holes, my skirt's split was *completely* split, and my shoes were scuffed. I just simply couldn't resist a good game of kickball or a foot race. Since my friend lived around the block, I would jump the fence to get to her house.

There was no doubt in my mind that I could be beautiful and girly one minute, and strong and fearless the next. If She-Ra could do it, so couldn't I. Let me refresh you about She-Ra. She was He-man's twin sister and the "Princess of Power." One moment she was gorgeous Princess Adora, but when she pulled out her sword, she became a heroine. This cartoon was my inspiration.

By the time I was ten years old, the tomboy in me had fully emerged. I began to hang out with the boys on my street who were two years my senior. I would tag along with them wherever they went. I became competitive and challenged them to everything from relay races to wrestling holds. I took a clothesline, and got right back up; I could escape a sleeper hold with ease, and my headlock was lethal. I loved to wrestle so much, I was going to try out for the team my freshman year of high school… or so I thought.

When my friend and I attempted to enter the gym, we were suddenly intercepted by the head coach. The words that came out of his mouth cut me as quickly and as deeply as a guillotine. He told us we had to be out of our minds if we thought he was going to let us on the team. Then he abruptly dismissed us and demanded we go back to class. I was hurt. At the time I was too young to understand that I was being discriminated against, nonetheless, the feelings were there. Had I known better, I would have taken up the issue with my principal, or even a higher authority. Unfortunately, I had not yet developed into the tenacious warrior that I am today.

Although the circumstances may vary, this type of thing still happens today. A girl loses her since of girl power because she is placed in a box by the rules and expectations of others. Often when this happens, it undermines a young girl's capabilities. All of a sudden, the world that is supposed to be her oyster snaps shuts on her. Sometimes it's one event, other times, it's a culmination of negative interactions that begin to make us feel like we need to surrender our inner She-Ra and liken ourselves to Snow White or Cinderella. When we compromise the essence of who we are, it becomes easier than taking the lead. By marching to someone else's tune, we aren't alienated because we're different; we belong. By becoming what we're *expected* to be, we don't disappoint anyone…except ourselves.

Being competitive, decisive, and outspoken is smiled on if you are male, but frowned down upon if you are female. I've always been the type of person who wanted to do it all, from putting on plays, to choreography, to writing novels, to fashion design. Whatever it was, I would emerge myself in it completely, and once I accomplished one goal, I was on to the next. As a young person, I viewed myself as bossy, domineering, scatter-brained, and hyperactive. Still, I didn't run from this, I owned it. What I learned as I matured and lived life a little, is that I am driven, passionate, goal-oriented, and in control of my destiny.

I personally don't think we struggle with figuring *who* we are as much as we struggle with *accepting* and not being afraid of who we are. Being a tomboy wasn't always easy. Sure R&B girl groups like Xscape and TLC rocked baggy men's clothes, but eventually even they became "Crazy, Sexy, Cool." My friends and I still were not ready. This meant that all of the guys loved us…as friends. We were the ones to call when they had girl problems, or wanted to discuss the NBA play offs. Sometimes I was left questioning myself when I liked a boy, and he in turn wanted me to hook him up with someone else. I think what helped me was that I had my girls who were in the same shoes, well, high top sneakers. We loved and supported one another, and our shared values forged a bond that would see us through more than two decades of victory and heartache. When one of us doubted the greatness in ourselves, we had each other to remind us. That is true girl power.

Unity definitely increases girl power. The more we uplift one other, the stronger we become, and this is passed from generation to generation. These words of advice are not just for daughters, but they are also for ourselves. As women, we must:

- Embrace our own individuality, and accept that of our "sisters." and "daughters." Seeing the beauty inside of you is a must, but just as important is seeing the beauty in others. There is no way I would have survived my teenage years without my girls in my corner.

- Encourage and support each other's endeavors. Remember that envy and jealously are not the same.
- This is a classic, if you don't have something good to say…you know the rest. An honest conversation with a close friend who asks your opinion is one thing, because you owe it to her to tell the truth. When a woman is trying to accomplish something, the last thing she needs to hear is a negative comment. Dreams are called dreams for a reason; it is not up to us to try to bring people down to reality.

This is especially for my daddies…

You potentially have the biggest impact on your daughter's abundance of, or lack of girl power. You are the first man to love your daughter, so if she ever feels rejected or neglected by you, it can scar her for life. However, if she is assured that Daddy has her back no matter what, she will know she can do any and everything.

My father had become a recent paraplegic at the time of my mother's passing, so I did not grow up living in the house with him. Nevertheless, when I needed an appendectomy at age 7, he was right there with a plush puppy for me (which I still have) as I was wheeled into surgery. My daddy has always seemed to take joy in his daughter's lively personality and ambitious endeavors. Knowing I had his unconditional love has been the safety net I've needed to walk the tight rope of dreams.

Losing…

Yourself

Sept.-1994 Wed. 11:15 am

On September 4, 1982, my mother died. I always thought that she died on the 23rd. I've been mourning her death every 23rd for the last eight to ten years. It's too late to change it this year, but I'll remember for sure next year. I'll just mourn Friday.

Every time I tell people that she's dead, they go, "Oh, I'm sorry." I don't feel sad much; only if someone talks about my mother, or if a family member talks about what she used to do. Everybody always says I'm built like her, got her attitude, her hands, her brains, I hope I don't grow up and have her breast cancer. But then again, I would hate for my sister to get it. I hate cancer. I hate how it took away so many people I loved. It hurt more when my grandmother died. I mean, she raised me for 10 years. Then she died on X-mas morning, of all days. I feel guilty because part of me wanted her to die. It seemed as if it were two of her: The healthy, happy, lovable, energetic, playful Ga-Ga, then there was the sick, skinny, short-haired, weak, incompetent Ga-Ga. I hated to watch her suffer, but I wanted her in my life. And I felt selfish, because I didn't want to suffer. I didn't want to watch her deteriorate. First she couldn't eat, her veins were broken down, so they couldn't feed her. She had to have pampers, and she could barely talk. A week before she died, she couldn't respond when we called her name.

Every night her hug got weaker and weaker, and every night I would pray that she lived to see Christmas. I meant the whole day, not just 'til morning. Then I was hurt that everybody at X-mas dinner pretended nothing had happened. I didn't even cry at her funeral, I watched everyone else cry, and some make spectacles of themselves. She was the foundation of our family. I'm going to her grave after school Friday. And to my mother's. It's going to be so hard, I haven't been there to see either of them since they were buried. It took me a long time to accept the fact that their bodies that are deteriorating in the ground, are not them. The real Ga-Ga and Brenda are in my heart and in my family's heart. Always.

2/26/95 2:25 pm

Lately, I've been thinking a lot about my Dad, probably because he's going to Florida for 2 weeks I've been thinking about my dad and my mom. I wanna know how he feels about her. Would they be together today if she were still alive? Or would they hate each other's guts? I wonder how he felt when she died. Did he stick by her while she was sick? Was he in love with her or was he a lying dog like most men? He probably was. But in my heart I hope and would like to think that they were hopelessly in love. That's because I'm a big dreamer. I would feel uncomfortable asking him about her. I mean, what if it was too painful for him to talk about? I don't want to bring back bad memories.

I feel bad when people talk about my mother, even if they are good things. Like yesterday, my aunt (my mother's sister) was saying that my other aunt (my father's sister) said that his new girlfriend was nice but no one can take the place of Brenda. That should make me feel good, the fact that my mother was so special. But it left me with an empty feeling inside, 'cause it's true, no one can take her place. I wonder what she'd being doing now if she were alive. Would she be successful? I think so. Everyone always talks about how smart and talented she was. How would she have been? What would she had *been? They always say how I look like her, I'm built like her. I'm supposed to have the same attitude as her, and be smart like her. I guess I'm kind of expected to live the life she would have lived. It's like it's my obligation and everyone's expectation. I don't mind, though. It's kind of an honor to be like my mother. I don't even feel comfortable saying mom, mommy, or ma 'cause I haven't said it since I was four. 3:35 pm*

P.S. I'm at work that's why it took so long to finish.

In May 2009, I lost a very good friend of mine to Leukemia. One day she called me on the phone and cried because she couldn't understand why I would call her, but I never came to see her. I tried to explain to her just how traumatizing it was for me to see someone I loved sick. The thought of seeing someone began the process of dwindling away brought back to the many horrific memories of Ga-Ga's illness. When my friend explained to me how lonely her sickness was at times, I had to push aside my own fears, and go see her.

Previously, in my mind, if I didn't see her sick, then she wasn't sick. Denial had worked for me as an adult. Going to her meant that I would have to come to terms with the fact that my friend at thirty-nine was fighting the battle of her life, for her life. Once I showed up at her house, her personality outshined her thinning hair, and her protective face mask. We talked and joked, and I was better off having faced my trepidation.

I only saw her once, because shortly after that she was in and out of the hospital and her immune system had grown weak. However, we still spoke on the phone quite often as she awaited a bone marrow transplant. One of her concerns was with her youngest daughter, who had just become a teenager. She couldn't understand why she had become so angry and distant towards her. Her little sweetheart now caused problems in the home and talked back to her in her condition.

As I heard her story, I empathized with her daughter. I assured her that she was acting out because she was afraid and hurt. I knew because I remembered when my grandmother became too sick to be the Ga-Ga that I needed; I also began acting out. I would yell back and argue with my younger aunts so much that I had to start staying at one of the older, sterner aunt's house. I didn't once think about the chaos or anxiety I caused my family;

nor did it ever occur to me that they were also suffering.

When we are teenagers, the world revolves around us (or so we think) and everything that happens good or bad, only affects our lives. When Ga-Ga passed away, I felt like I was the only one who'd lost her; I didn't think that so did my sister. I didn't think about the fact that my aunts had lost a mother, or my great aunts had lost a sister. She was my Ga-Ga and I was the one who was in anguish.

I remember I got a diary on that Christmas morning. This would be the first time I would began to put my thoughts on paper. It was one of those small diaries, with the flap that locked closed with a set of gold keys. I don't know whatever happened to that particular diary, but I remember its first entry; it was angry. I remember writing that I wanted to scream at all of the adults in the room, "She's dead! She's dead! Stop pretending to be happy!"

While that was one of the worst days of my life, something wonderful came from it. From then on, I began to document my emotions constantly. So while no one knew how depressed I really was, I could always confide in my diary, and when that was full, I had notebooks, or loose leaf paper, or the back of fast food tray liners. From the journal writing came poetry. I cannot for the life of me remember my first poem, but I know it was about Ga-Ga, and it poured out of me like unshed tears. Writing would eventually become my therapy, and the one thing that would keep me from spiraling completely out of control.

After Ga-Ga was gone, I shut myself down emotionally for the next few years. The only things that kept me sane were the poetry and short stories; the only thing that made me happy was dance. Other than that, I felt I had no purpose. I had no desire.

Like a programmed robot, I systemically marched through my adolescent years: school, work and home. I made the honor roll, I participated in after-school activities, and hung out with friends. To the outside world, I was your average high school student. But inside, I was desolate, a candle whose flame had been blown out. I did things because I was expected to do them, not because I wanted to.

Of all people, teenagers seem to take the loss of others the hardest. Younger children are more accepting. My guess is because they don't fully grasp the concept. Particularly hard, is when you lose a peer. Eight months after my grandmother died, I lost someone I referred to as my cousin. You know how it is, when families become intertwined after generations are friends, and their children have children with each other? Well, we were raised together like family, and he was just thirteen years old when he died from a gunshot wound. His funeral was so traumatizing that I vowed to never attend another again, and I meant it.

The following year, I was a freshman in high school and a classmate of mine was hit by a drunk driver while riding in the car with his mother. To me, it was easier to pretend he moved away, then to go to his funeral and see him lying there.

When my friend Carrie died less than two weeks before our junior prom, I again avoided going to her service. If I didn't witness her coffin inside of a church, or visit her burial site, then she wasn't dead, she just moved away.

Carrie, too had died in a car accident, but this time it was while riding with our peers. I'd known her since elementary school, and she and I always had the same English and Spanish classes. One day, instead of watching a movie the teacher was showing, we talked about who we were going to the prom with, and what we were wearing. Less than a week later, she was gone.

To cope with death, I numbed myself to emotion, and focused on schoolwork, finding a job, or drowning myself in alcohol (See *Experimenting with Danger*). Death became my enemy, and I felt like I won a battle if I didn't show up and accept that someone was gone. To further antagonize him, I would taunt and tease death by putting myself in perilous situations; test him, secretly wishing he'd win and take me away from my misery.

It wasn't until my senior year that my fire for life was re-ignited by my Psychology and African-American History teacher. She saw something in me that I didn't see in myself. This teacher made me want to learn again and she made me feel special. Each day for two classes periods, she captivated me with her knowledge, and comforted me her kindness. To me, she was fascinating; beautiful and smart, honest and caring. I would find myself sitting at her desk, waiting to share with her the details of my day. I was reaching out, something I hadn't done since Ga-Ga was alive. In her, I got the reassurance, confidence boosts, and guidance that I had been lacking. There was something about her warm spirit that made me feel good inside, that made me reach for goals for myself and not just for others.

While I was in college, I wrote her a letter telling her how influential she was to me. She had no idea that she'd made so much of an impact on my life in such a short period of time.

That's the thing about working with young people…sometimes you never know how much your time, love and support means to them until later. When you're that young person, you often don't realize how that adult is really changing your life.

Despite that teacher making me find my light again, I was still unable to visit the cemetery until I was nineteen years old. I remember going there on Mother's day, kneeling down, and crying uncontrollably at my mother and grandmother's headstones. This was the day that I truly began healing.

More than a decade later, I still have my moments where I feel the loss, wishing I could curl up in the bed with Ga-Ga and fall asleep with her. Other times I wish I could ask her or my mom for advice, just to see what they would say. What helps through these hard times, are the good times. In my heart I believe that sometimes they are right beside me, cheering me on as I cross the finish line of each goal. When it gets too hard, I focus on doing something positive in their memory to remind me that their legacy can continue through me.

My mother, my father and me

My Mother

Me and my Ga-Ga

CAUTION!
ELECTRICALLY
OPERATED PRODUCT

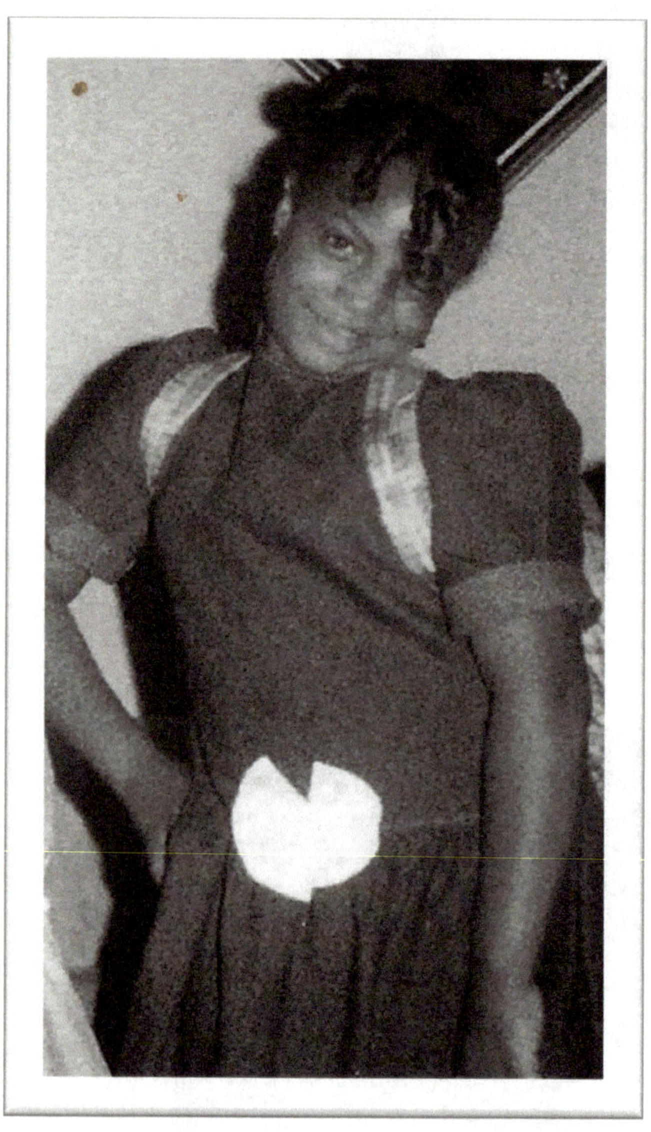

The first day of school for 3rd grade

Pound Cake

Friday/Saturday 1995

12:15 am

...and today Jabari had his arm around my waist. It made me feel uncomfortable because wondered if he felt my rolls hanging out on the sides. Oh my goodness, I need to start shaping up for the summer so I can look sexy and stuff. Starting tomorrow, word up, I gotta get back on track with exercising.

10:00 pm April 10, 1995

Dear Diary,

Correct me if I'm wrong, but right now, I should be happy. The event I've been waiting for since the summer is just 17 days away, but I can't seem to find the right dress, and it's depressing me. So is my weight. I haven't thought about it in a while, but lately the insults have been thrown at me a lot. I'm trying to starve but my attempt has become very unsuccessful. And when I look in the mirror (especially in dressing rooms) I want to die. I look so large. I HATE MY BODY. It's really sucky. For some reason, I want to look flawless in 17 days, but that's impossible because I'm large, everybody knows it, just some try not to say it. That's it, from now on, until Thursday, I don't eat. That's final. I gotta lose weight. I'm gross.

Toya B

Preparing for my junior prom should have been exciting for me, not mortifying. But like many teenage girls, I had major body image issues. Young women of color today have it a lot easier than before, I think. While the modeling industry standards remain unrealistic and idiotic, we have seen a recent embracing of curves by celebrities like Beyoncé, Shakira, Alicia Keys, and just about every "Reality Star".

When I was an adolescent, I couldn't say that I saw someone on TV who looked like me until Janet Jackson came on the scene. She was pretty, talented, and had a real body. Then from one CD to the next, I saw this dancing tomboy turn into a goddess with the flattest stomach I had ever seen. I watched in awe as Janet strolled along the beach in the *Love will Never Do* video. I was mystified, while feeling somewhat betrayed. There were no more blazers and turtle necks, now it was all about the midriff. What did that mean to me? It meant that the magazines and videos were right, skinny was in, and thick, chunky, fat (whatever you want to call it) was out. It meant that instead of going outside and being a kid, I first had to do *Bodies in Motion with Gilad* or one of Denise Austin's latest workout videos. At eleven I deprived myself of *Captain Crunch* in exchange for Corn Flakes because they had fewer calories.

Calories?
At age eleven?
Yes!

Looking back at the photos of me doing the teapot pose (you know, hands on the waist, leaning over to one side) I was not a fat child. I was by no means skinny, but I had a solid build with very muscular legs. None of that mattered, because I wasn't what I saw on TV. Even Vanessa Williams with the same green eyes and honey colored hair, who made me feel good about my different looks, was slim.

My troubles with body acceptance continued. When I was thirteen, I suffered from strep throat and lost ten pounds in a week. Then came the compliments. I had lost weight and people told me, "It looks good." My family noticed, my friends at school, and more importantly, I noticed. So, in my mind, I had discovered a new diet plan…only drink liquids and eat soft foods, like instant mashed potatoes with water, and I could maintain my weight loss and perhaps even drop a few more pounds. No one in my family had any idea that I dieted. I ate regularly at dinner time, so my secret wouldn't be discovered. It was easy to cover up the fact that I wasn't eating because all of the adults in the house were preoccupied by my grandmother's losing fight with cancer. When she finally succumbed to her illness, I lost my desire to exercise and searched for solace in Little Debbie snack cakes. Within five months of her passing, I had gained back those fifteen pounds. That, my newly formed body courtesy of puberty, and the fact that I would be entering high school prompted me to find another, more extreme method for weight loss. In the summer of 1992, I began the ice and water diet.

When my friends questioned why I didn't want any Swedish fish or Stateline Barbeque Chips, I blamed it on the summer heat. For a week and a half my caloric intake was less than 500 daily. In front of people I would sip on a juice, or take bites of food here and there. It was so easy to fool everyone, and it essentially made me feel powerful in a world where I had recently began to feel powerless.

Two factors caused me to abandon my ice and water diet. First, I was feeling so weak I could barely accomplish all that I was used to doing in my busy day. The second thing was the upcoming Labor Day picnic. How could I explain to either side of my family that I didn't want macaroni and cheese or ribs? It would surely draw attention. I would have to be content with shopping for size 9/10 jeans when I went school shopping. This struggle would go on for almost ten more years.

It wasn't until I was in my mid- twenties and at my heaviest- 237 pounds, that I finally began to accept my stretch marks, fat rolls, and cellulite. I wrote a poem called. Mirror, Mirror, I Don't Need You and dubbed myself "The Queen of Self-Esteem." I strutted across the stage during poetry performances, celebrating my body, and really loving myself from head to toe.

When I began to lose weight, it was by accident. I wanted to try this new exercise…Pilates. One class and I was hooked. After a month, I had lost about 10 pounds, without even dieting. Then I began to think, well, what if I tried to get healthy, instead of losing weight? I could reduce my chances of the hereditary diseases that were in my family: high blood pressure, Type II diabetes, and cancer. I made some small changes in my food habits, experimented with a few more classes, and before I knew it, I was back to my high school senior weight.

Now when I look back at myself in size 18 jeans, still doing the teapot pose, I see how I glowed with confidence. I had gotten past the point where everyone else's standards no longer mattered. Today, as woman in her thirties, I am sixty pounds lighter, and anyone who knew me a few years ago will say I didn't seem "that big." That's because I flaunted my meaty figure. Today, I still flaunt my size 10 (sometimes comfortably, and sometimes not so much) and like any woman, I have my sexy days, and my fat days. The difference is I am no longer consumed with thoughts of numbers on a scale, pants size, or diet fads. I exercise because it feels good, not because I want to look like Jenifer Beal's body double in *Flashdance*.

It wasn't the media alone that shaped how I should view my body. It was being told in 6th grade that my grey pants suit made me look like an elephant. It was being taunted by my uncle about not being able to beat my sister in a foot race because being so big made me slow. It was being told by my so-called best friend at twelve that my crush wouldn't like me back because even though I had I cute face, I was flat-chest and I needed to lose weight. It was another friend who explained to me that the reason I didn't have stretch marks like she did was because I was meant to be fat so my skin didn't need to be stretched.

My point in all this is that the world is cold enough without parents and loved ones making it colder. Your child should not be on a diet, nor be told that she needs to go on one! You are her first line of defense against negative body images. There are too many creative ways to ensure your child leads a healthy lifestyle. Exercise can be camouflaged in dance, jump rope, and sports. Healthy food habits start at home with you. You cannot feed your child processed food, juice boxes, and chips for 8 years and then suddenly become health conscious, or what I like to call fat conscious; it's hypocritical. It's up to you to teach your child about portion control and drinking enough water. We play secret agents all of the time to disguise cough medicine, why can't we do the same for fruits, veggies, and protein?

The other part of securing a growing girl's self-acceptance is following the same order you often find yourself shouting, "Watch your mouth!" Whoever coined that phrase about sticks and stones hurting and words not, didn't know a damn thing. The human body is amazing in its capacity to heal external wounds, especially in young people. But internal wounds are much more complicated. As adults, we can't remember every time we scraped a knee or tripped on a stair. However, many of us can recall the teasing, the cruel nicknames, and in some cases, the bullying.

Not only is it wrong to constantly remind your child of their weight or deprive them of treats, but that's how people end up hiding food, or binging and purging. What's equally important is that you have a positive body image. When your child hears you call yourself fat, or constantly talking about diets, she can internalize this and eventually develop a warped perspective of what is attractive. It's like baking a cake, too much of one thing, and not enough of the other can destroy the outcome.

Experimenting with Danger

March 6, 1994 11:03 pm

Me and Shay went downtown to Tyrone's house and got potted and drunk off of a gosher and 40...

It was a spontaneous night 'cause we told Shay's mother we were going to McDonald's, but we went looking for a party. Some fat dude tried to kick it to us on the street. We (me, Shay, and Tina) got in the car with two Puerto Rican guys from Bridgeport, CT to help them with directions. In return they gave us beer. You know I f___ed mine up...

Sun. /Mon. June 4/5 12:14am

Dear Diary,

Friday I got so blasted off Southern Comfort, gin, and 151 proof. I was at Robby's house with Haji (the one who was driving when Carrie died) and Tommy and Shena. Robby graduated last year. I challenged Tommy to a drink off and won. But then I was throwing up all on Robby's floor and in his trash. I felt like I was regurgitating my whole liver, and even though I don't really know Haji, he was right there holding my hand, rubbing my back and my stomach, saying he wasn't gonna leave me. I think he felt sorry for me because of what happened to Carrie. Whatever the case, he was sweet. It was crazy, I remember we started drinking right when the Pacers started playing; it was like 7:30. By like 8, I was down. I was in and out of a daze for four hours. I threw up on my shirt. Robby had to give me a new one. He kept giving me everything I asked for, and he didn't even kick me out. I kept hearing Shena say it was time to go home, even though she was drunk, too. And I felt Tommy holding my hand and kissing my forehead, saying I was gonna be okay. I think he was drunk, too. Then Haji dipped, nobody knows where he went. I snuck in the house after 2:30. Then yesterday when I went to take my SAT's, I felt like sh*t. As a matter of fact, I threw up, right in the room, on the desk, on my answer sheet, in front of 30 people. I wasn't even embarrassed, I didn't give a damn. Now I have to take the exam in October, but I wanted to take it now! I was pissed, and my aunt suspected I was drinking. I told her some mess about the Raspberry Lemonade I drank. Yuck!

Latoya B.

I had my first drink of alcohol at fourteen, right underneath the roof where I dwelled. My three girlfriends and I were bored, so we decided to check out the liquor cabinet where my aunt's husband kept scotch-whiskey, gin, and vodka. We poured a little of each into a punch bowl and mixed it with some Kool-Aid. An hour later we were on the city bus, on our way to the mall. This was just the beginning of five more years of putting ourselves in dangerous situations. I am still slightly disturbed when I look back on all of my risky behavior involving alcohol. I've gotten in the car with teens that were under the influence, despite losing two classmates (one of them was Carrie) in catastrophic drunk driving accidents. Countless times I came home completely wasted, and undetected.

Young people start to drink for many reasons. For me, alcohol was a temporary escape from reality; I didn't have to worry about yesterday or tomorrow. I even knew my limits; I was a peer educator, trained in teaching others about drugs and alcohol, but I would always push my limits. I literally didn't care if I lived or died. Life was not important to me after my grandmother's passing. I was a walking contradiction. I would straighten up, reduce the drinking if my grades slipped because I wanted to go to college, but then on Friday I'd be cheering on a classmate from the backseat while he drag raced another student. My spiritual side tells me that I survived these foolish incidents because I have a greater purpose…to potentially save lives with my story.

One Saturday before Easter and shortly after my sixteenth birthday, I had an experience that made me quit drinking beer for about fifteen more years. Up until then I could go to the corner liquor store and buy a forty ounce for

$1.10. I'd sit at the park with Shena and we'd drink and chat.

This particular night one of my good male friends came by with three other guys. In the backseat were twelve forty ounces of *Old English* beer, we found a side street to park on few blocks away. Lance rolled up two goshers (cigars) with marijuana, and we commenced to drinking and smoking. Being the only female around a group of guys, my competitive nature crept up on me and I felt like I had to do my share and drink three bottles. I did it in about an hour. Now that I'm a teacher I want to do the math:

40 ounces x 3 = 120 ounces of beer.
One serving of beer = 12 ounces
120 / 12 = 10 servings of alcohol

That's right, I had ten drinks in an hour….alcohol poisoning. The driver of the car, also had the equivalent of ten drinks. I sat back and relaxed as he drove me home. I never thought twice about what could have happened with him operating a vehicle under that condition, or what could have happened if these guys weren't my friends and decided to take sexual advantage of me.

I made it home safely, and after kissing one of the boys (whom I never liked, but once again it was just me being foolish and uninhibited.) Then I staggered to my back door, only to realize, I didn't have my key. I knew my sister and my cousin were home, but it was after 1:00 a.m. so they were dead to the world. Still I began banging loudly; there was no answer.

My body could no longer handle the over dose of poison and I began to vomit right outside my front door…all beer. Then to make matters worse, I also urinated on myself; my body was trying to shut down. I lived in a side by side housing complex, and my sister's bedroom faced the front side. I ran clumsily along the rows of apartments and around to front side of my street. I threw pebbles at her window and shouted her name…no answer. I ran once again around to back, falling in dirt, which stuck to my soaked jeans.

At this point my head was spinning, and I just wanted the bed. I began banging on the back door again. This time my uncle, who lived next door came outside. I straightened up and explained to him that I had just come from the movies and I didn't have my key. He had no clue that I was drunk out of my mind when he directed me to sleep at his place for the night. I passed out in my cousin's bed, and changed her sheets the next morning. The whole next day, I experienced what it meant to have a hangover. Headache and nausea were my biggest concerns. Not once did I reflect on how many different ways I could have died the night before, from an accident to alcohol poisoning.

What can we learn from all of this? Though I never got busted, I know for sure that no amount of threats or punishments can stop a teenage girl from experimenting with drugs and alcohol. Just think back to your junior high and high school days. How many of us passed a joint or shared a pint of cheap liquor at a party or after school? Sometimes the mere reflections on these times scare us when we look at our daughter and say, "Wow, she's fifteen. When I was fifteen, I was getting drunk on weekends." It's a harsh reality that cannot be ignored.

Just as equally harmful is lying about your use. I mean, how do you explain yourself when she finds the picture of you and her godmother smoking on a bong after you told her you never tried marijuana? What's a parent to do? Do you tell them hangover horror stories? Not a great idea. I told mine just this one, again, for the purpose of opening eyes and saving lives. Do you scare them with facts about how dangerous alcohol is and how it harms your health? Not a good look if two days later she witnesses you entertaining your girlfriends with martini's and margaritas. Besides, just like me, they learn the facts in school. Again, I'm no expert, but experience tells me you should be appropriately honest with your child. I can't tell you when these talks should happen because it should be ongoing. I can tell you that your approach should be open and have set boundaries:

- You are an adult and legally allowed to drink. However keep in mind that you are being watched, so you must do so responsibly.
- Set clear rules. You cannot control what your child does outside of your house, but there needs to be an understanding that alcohol consumption will not be allowed in the home.
- Prepare your child in the instance that she does choose to drink. She should know to never sip from a drink prepared by someone else, and to never leave a drink unattended.
- It is critical that she and her friends stay together at parties. I recommend a "designated friend" This is someone who will be perfectly able to notify parents or 911 in case of an emergency, while doing her best to ensure that her friends don't make decisions they may later regret.
- Though I feel hypocritical even as I write this, you must reiterate over and over that under no circumstances should she ever get in the car with someone who has had even one drink. One fatal flaw young people tend to have is the thought that they are invincible and immortal; it just won't happen to them.

Drug and alcohol experimentation is not 100% preventable. However, the chances of your child being involved in life-threatening situations can be greatly decreased if you arm them with education and the security that they can openly communicate with you about these issues.

Not like the Movies

Sunday Feb., 1994 10:10pm

Yo,

I called Man last night. I was scared to because I thought he would be mad 'cause I didn't come over, well, he wasn't. I lied to him; I told him I went out of town at the last minute with one of my friends and her mother because I didn't have nothing to do over vacation. Man said, "I coulda found something for you to do." And you know what he meant...

Okay, I'm back, the phone rang and it was him. I stopped writing while we were talking. Like I was saying, Man was talking about sex. But I know I don't mean anything to him. I'm not risking my virginity for somebody who don't care about me. "I don't see nothing wrong with a little bump and grind" but some love has to be behind it all. Word is born!

I know that if me and him have sex, I'll fall in love with him. But it'll be my first time and I don't wanna regret that. If Man wants this, he's gonna have to work for it!

Latoya (Toya B)

10:58 pm

July 25, 1994
Dear Diary,

Oh God! Let me tell you about Man. I don't know if I told you already, but on July 21, we kissed, and so did Shena and Jordan. Everything was honky dory, until Friday. We did our dance routine and got back around midnight. Man called, I was souped. He wanted me to go over Jordan's house with Shena on Saturday. We told them how neither of our parents knew we were home yet. So they met us outside Bobby's apartment. Were they showing off? Of course. Shena and Jordan ended up breaking up cause he wanted to "f**k" (his exact words) and so they cut each other off. He knew he was sorry as soon as he said it. And Man...he sat next to me the whole time and didn't say nothing. We were watching Ace Ventura, and I dozed off for a minute. Bobby was like, "Did you come here to go to sleep or talk to Man?" I didn't answer. Then his boy Chase was like, "I have a question, too."

I told him I didn't want to hear it, but Man said he did. So then Chase asks,
"Do you be f**kin' ?" I said no, so him and Bobby hissed at me and gave Man that, "Put her out if she ain't puttin; out" look. Then Shena comes out of the kitchen, and
Jordan comes out too and says, " Yo, if you see me

talking to her, hit me." Shena was like, "Let's go." Man was like, "That's right, 'cause ya services are no longer needed." I was so pissed off and shocked that I grabbed the first thing I saw, a brush and I threw it at him. It hit him and he started talking sh*t, saying he would fight me. I stepped to him, but he didn't do anything. So I was like, "Schmuck!" and I slammed the door on my way out. Me and Shena was heated, boy. You couldn't tell us nothing.

If they want to get in our pants, they are gonna have to come better than that, like with some respect. Did they really think they were gonna get screwed in a house full of dudes? Try again. Man better go find somebody else to bang with, I had enough of him.

I told Lance about it, and he said that man was dead wrong...duh!

Peace out,
Toyab

9/13/94

I guess my mind is still in a flutter. Last time wrote you I was, at least I thought I was in a happy relationship with Nick. But he blew it when he asked for...sex. Na, baby, I'm not gonna be able to do it. I didn't quite get around to dumping him yet. I thought I'd just let him figure it out...

16-Sept-1994 Fri. 11:14am

... And Nick still doesn't get the picture yet, he still keeps talking about ... sex, sex, sex, sex, sex, and more sex. It's quite annoying. He's about to piss me off to the highest point. I'm about to just tell him to take a long walk off a short pier.

My closest circle of friends and I referred to ourselves as the Virgin Posse. We would be different from the rest of the girls in school because we didn't have sex. Now there was no pledge to be celibate or wait until marriage, we just valued our treasure and vowed to share it only when we were completely ready. It was imperative that we "did it" with someone we loved. Some of my friends stayed members of the virgin posse until college. I denounced my membership on September 23, 1995.

Depending on your age, you may or may not remember the seven minute Betty Wright song, *Tonight is the Night (You Make Me Your Woman*). It was about a young woman losing her virginity, and I listened to it on repeat the night I yielded mine. It happened so quickly; one minute I was on the phone with him, the next he was at my door and I was sneaking him down the stairs into the secrecy of my basement bedroom.

I met him when I was just fifteen years old in the summer of 1993; he was seventeen at the time. By August, I was in love. Some people would argue me down about young people not knowing love, but even now being older and more experienced, I can honestly say, what I felt was real. He was no different from the others guys around my way in terms of appearance, or personality, but the way I felt about him was different, and new.

For the next two years, on and off, he and I would talk on the phone, kiss, or hang out with the other kids who lived in or near my housing projects. He, being a typical young male, periodically tried to get me to go "all the way." I wouldn't budge. My virginity was much too valuable to me, and once I relinquished it, I would never get it back.

I'm not quite sure where this strong conviction came from, but my guess is my Ga-Ga. I never had anyone sit me down to officially discuss "the birds and the bees." Everything I learned about sex had come from a peer education program I participated in from ninth to eleventh grade. I was well informed about condoms, STD's and body parts. However, this didn't stop other teens that were equally trained from having unprotected sex. Therefore, I attribute my feelings about waiting to feeling loved and valued while I was growing up.

Even with my insecurities regarding my weight and being a tomboy, my self-esteem never faltered. Self-esteem is a word used loosely and interchangeably with confidence, but there is a difference. Confidence entails believing in your capabilities, abilities or appearance. Esteem has to do with recognizing your value as in individual. A woman can be confident because of her brick house body, beautiful face, and the right pair of heels. However, if she sleeps around with men in search of love, then she may be lacking self-esteem.

Though at fifteen I wasn't aware of it, I had a feeling of importance that my grandmother instilled in me with every hug, every home cooked meal, and every single word of encouragement. Therefore, no one had to caution me to wait to have sex, I knew I wasn't going to give up "my stuff" to just anyone.

Believe me, there were boys always trying to coax me out of my panties. Whenever one of my "boyfriends" proposed sex, I was instantly turned off, especially if I felt like he didn't ask correctly. Any use of vulgar language, like the "f" word, or the "p" word immediately eliminated an applicant's chances of winning my prize. Yes, I said prize.

I don't know why I finally said yes that night. Maybe it was because I was in my senior year of high school, and I felt I was grown. Maybe it was because my aunt was out of town on her honeymoon, and I knew her sister, who was looking after us, slept like a rock. Maybe I was just ready. Whatever the reason, when he called me that Sunday night and asked when I would make time to see him. I told home whenever he wanted me to, and responded with, "What if I said I wanna see you now?"

My reply was, “I’d say gimme twenty minutes?” I surprised myself as soon as I said it. I think even he was shocked to hear me be suggestive after trying for two and a half years.

Needless to say, when we hung up, I began my preparations. I pressed play on my boom box, and sang along with Betty, and feeling the lyrics, “I’m nervous, and I’m trembling, waiting for you to walk in…” I had to be sure I smelled nice, and had on my cute bra, that he would never see because the room would be pitch black. When he called to tell me he was outside, I changed the latest tape from Jodeci, *I Wanna Freak You.*

Fifteen minutes later, it was all over and I was no longer a member of the Virgin Posse. The whole time I kept saying to myself, “I can’t believe I’m doing it.” I was so excited that about telling my best friend the next day at school, that I forgot to focus on trying to find some pleasure in it.

As with every relationship, we all have regrets, but I choose to focus on the positive. For me, it was that I was in control of the situation. I didn’t allow myself to succumb to the pressure of having sex after getting drunk at a party, or in some stranger’s bed. It was my home court, and I called all the shots. I didn’t lose my virginity, no one took it, it was something I chose to give to someone I cared about, at a time in my life when I felt I was comfortable.

Whether you’re an adult or a teenager, sex is complicated. In my work and personal experience, I’ve witnessed parents address the topic across the spectrum. Some use fear of pregnancy, STD’s, or eternal damnation. Some, and I think this is the worst, actually ignore the topic. They lie to themselves about the possibility of their child having sex at thirteen, and only face the truth when it smacks them in the face.

Recently I’ve seen parents try to be cool and speak candidly about sex with their children. However, this can backfire, embarrassing your child and shutting her down completely. Rewind to when you were fifteen. It doesn’t matter what type of relationship you have or had with your mother. Chances are you wince at the thought of discussing the messiness of sex with her.

You and your daughter's personalities and personal experiences will ultimately determine the best approach. What is most important is that your daughter has a knowledgeable, nonjudgmental and trusting adult she can go to anytime to talk. If it happens to be your sister or a family friend, you need to understand that even though it is your child, you don't have to know everything. While this may be hard to swallow, you have to trust that the adult your daughter chooses will value confidentiality, but prioritize safety.

When I became sexually active, I had the youngest of my mother's sisters, who was so blunt, so insightful, that all of my friends went to her, too. She gave me the hard core facts, candidly speaking about everything from the lies guys would perpetuate to get what they want, to oral sex, to birth control. Talking with her gave all of the clinical information I was learning some human relatability. With no topic being taboo, I felt safe asking important questions.

Sex is scary, especially when you're a young girl, but probably more so when you're the parent of a young girl. I like to use a metaphor of teaching your child how to ride a bike. She needs to learn the parts and how they work, and then become confident and comfortable. Eventually you have to take off the training wheels, let go of the back of the seat, and hope that she goes at the right speed and keeps her balance. If she should fall, have faith that you gave all she needs to pick herself up, and be there for her, in case she does need a little help.

At 13, hiding my grief behind the smile

Conclusion (For Now)

Adolescence was one of the most traumatic and magnificent times of my life. I wouldn't change any of my experiences for the world, because each one, great and small, ugly or beautiful, tragic or triumphant, has helped to shape the fabulous woman I've become. That's right, I said fabulous. Simply because I didn't allow my circumstances to define me. There were times over the years where I became temporarily lost, but still, I always dreamed of great things for myself.

In my field of work I often see a population without hope. Either they don't believe they will live long enough to have a future, or they don't believe in their own greatness to have a fulfilling future. It's hard to see past the pain, the neglect, the violence of the past, so they just let it consume them. For some of the young people I work with, there is no sunshine after the rain.

I flourished despite the cloudy forecast because I was raised with love. Even with losing important people, I was always cared for adoringly. Not for one second could I imagine growing up without that security, but many children do. It's mighty hard to love yourself when no one else sees any value in you.

When I was oblivious to the love that still surrounded me after my Ga-Ga's death, poetry became my salvation. While I believe that anyone can be a poet, it may not be for everyone. What is important though, is that each and everyone of us, adults and children alike, have a healthy outlet. Be it sports, art, dance, or music, we need to be able to release all of the emotion that can potentially destroy our spirits. Although I wasn't aware at the time, poetry became my therapy.

The last ingredient that was necessary for my growth was having a mentor. Maybe I'm wrong in this generalization, but I notice that adolescents get to a point in their development where they pull away from parents and caregivers, and look toward their friends for life's answers. A mentor is that balance; they are relatable like a peer, but adult enough to know better. They offer advice without chastising, and can open our eyes to new thinking and experiences. My mentors have changed over the years, but that high school teacher was by far one of the people who came into my life at right time. It's no coincidence that I turned out to be a teacher; she inspired me.

I said it in the beginning, and I'll say it again, I don't have all the answers. I can only speak from my experience, tell my story. What I know is that the above three things were the roots, the sunshine, and water that enabled me to blossom into the woman I am today. So it is with conviction that I say, it is our responsibility to bestow upon young girls everywhere these intangible, vital gifts so that they may bloom no matter the weather. Shine on.

Always,
Brenda's Child

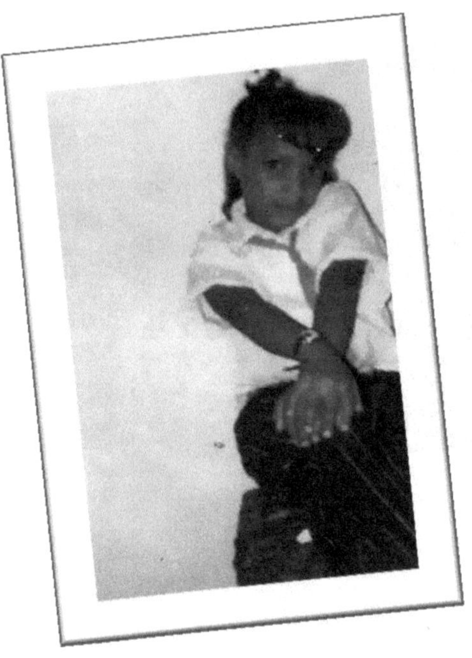

My roots, my water, and my sunshine…Ga-Ga

Don't Block My Sunshine

Why can't I be great?
Have everything I want in life?
Do whatever I find gratifying?
Be free to explore every possibility?
Why do I have to be small enough to fit
in the box you designed for me?
Be limited
by your narrow definitions and categories?
That exclude instead of describe.

Dreams are called dreams for a reason,
So don't diminish mine with your reality.
I have enough of a challenge
trying to please me,
to make myself feel happy and complete,
I don't have the extra energy
to spend on keeping you happy,
especially when you'll never truly be.

You're spending too much time
trying to keep me insignificant and tiny
when I'm destined for greatness.
I can't be molded into your likeness.
So please don't try to shape me…
Just let me be.
Fuel me with support,
Encouragement and kindness,
Or kindly…step to the side,
Because I don't need your darkness,
Blocking my sunshine!

Tell 'em Why You Shine

I've been told I love attention…
well duh!
But I don't need it, and I don't seek it
like you proclaim,
it just follows me wherever I go,
charisma some call it,
shine others use to define
the fact that I stand out
never lost in the background,
There's no motive,
but there is rhyme (since I'm poet)
and reason…
it's because I TRY
You can't help but to catch people's eye
when you strive
for your dreams while others stand by
on the sidelines.

This is why I shine.
And I won't apologize
that my confidence level is high,
It should be …
because I know what I'm of capable of
and I love
my tenacity,
so excuuuuse me
if a spotlight seems to follow me
on my journey,
but you wouldn't be so blinded
by my shimmer,
so offended by my brilliant bright,
if you chased your dreams,
and walked in your own light.

My Purpose

My purpose in life is to use my story as a testimony
So those in the darkness can see that
There is no such thing as excuses or limits
Restrictions or boundaries
It starts with acceptance, and self-love
Which leads to confidence,
Then anything can be accomplished.

My great daddy was a sharecropper,
My grandma a maid,
My mother had me at 19
And I gave birth to my first son at the same age.
Like her I was on Medicaid,
Lived in subsidized apartments
Paid 40 dollars a month for rent, thanks to section 8.
A decade later I had a master's degree,
Bought my own home, on my own,
I guess you can call it a the UNdeferred dream
I've experienced and seen both poverty and financial stability
Driven off lots with brand new cars
And had to get jumpstarts on hoop-tees
But none of this defines me
No amount of money, schooling or extensive vocabulary
Can dictate my worth
Like Maya Angelou said. "You may shoot me with your words,
You may cut me with your eyes"
And yes it does hurt,
But because my ancestor's prayed for me... centuries
Before my birth
Like her and the many others before me "Still I rise"

And it should come as no surprise that

My purpose in life is to use my story as a testimony
So those in the darkness can see that
There is no such thing as excuses or limits
Restrictions or boundaries

My past is significant
It shaped me, but it doesn't define me
The world owes me no favors
Because I suffered awful tragedies.
As a matter of fact I owe it to my mother and her mother to continue their legacy
Of love, encouragement and stern nurturing

I must lead by example and set high expectations
For those who don't recognize their potential, their magnificence,
I'll quote Maya again,
"She stands in the classroom loving children into understanding"
That's me,
This is my burden but it's more of a blessing
I'm the wounded healer.
learning about myself, while teaching life lessons.

About the Author

Brenda's Child has made it her life's mission to inspire people through poetry and stories and through leading by example with courage, confidence, and integrity.

Born Latoya Bosworth, she dubbed herself Brenda's Child at the age of 21, in honor of her late mother Brenda Kay Swinton. Brenda's Child is the confident diva, with a smooth spoken word style. She uses her poetry as an outlet as she experiences the daily joys and struggles of being a mother, youth advocate, teacher, African-American, female, optimist, and dream seeker.

In April of 2007 Brenda's Child self-published her first book of poetry entitled A Piece of My Mind...Poetic Confessions of a Self-Proclaimed Diva.
Since then she has published several titles of various genres, all centered around H.E.R.S (Health, Empowerment, Resiliency and Self-Esteem).

Brenda's Child, or Miss Toya, as she called by "her kids" is also a Freedom Writer teacher, mentor and motivational speaker. She completed her B.A in Sociology with a minor in Social Work from Western New England University in 2002, and her M.S. in Nonprofit Management and Philanthropy at Bay Path University in 2009. She has myriad of human service experience, particularly with at-risk youth and families. Over the last 14 years, she has worked in programs affiliated with the Department of Children and Families, and Department of Youth Services. She has also implemented curriculum for after school programs and summer camps, and facilitated workshops for youth and youth workers. In 2006 she established Keep Youth Dreaming and Striving (KYDS), a nonprofit mentoring program. She is currently completing her dissertation for her PhD in Human Services. For more information visit:

www.brendaschild.com

www.myshine.info

www.mykyds.org